How William Met Mommy

Written by Tracey Adams
Illustrated by Gaurav Bhatnagar

How William Met Mommy
Written by Tracey N. Adams

Illustrations by Gaurav Bhatnagar

Published by Pa-Pro-Vi Publishing
www.paprovipublishing.com

ISBN:978-1-959667-59-9

Printed in the United States of America

This story is dedicated to Mommy and William.
May they continue to rest in eternal peace.

It was a sad day for Tracey and her siblings. They had to say goodbye to their precious mother. She meant the world to them, and they were going to miss her terribly.

They all came to terms that Mommy was no longer with them here on earth. However, they all knew she would forever live in their hearts.

They knew she was going to a beautiful place where there was no pain, no suffering. Mommy left them with her wisdom, her strength, and with butterflies!

Butterflies! Mommy loved butterflies! She had butterfly decorations in her house! She wanted a butterfly tattoo! Now, she visits her children as a beautiful butterfly. Butterflies, like people, go through a metamorphosis! A transition. The change, the metamorphosis, life, can be challenging however, the transition is beautiful. Just like a butterfly.

It was another glorious day in Heaven. William thought that Heaven looked so much like earth except in Heaven the streets were paved in pure gold. There were beautiful mansions that sparkled on their own.

There were meadows and gardens and rainbows everywhere. The mountains were way bigger than the ones on earth and instead of snow-capped mountains, Heaven's mountain caps had silver whipped crème and they sparkled constantly.

It was never nighttime in Heaven. On earth, the sun provided the sunlight, whereas in Heaven, it was God's presence and pure glory that provided the light. Everyone was happy and smiling in Heaven and no one ever got sick!

The angels flew around singing and dancing and praising constantly. The sound was nothing like William had ever heard.

The flowers and trees never died and there was always a sweet smell that permeated throughout the heavenly air. William thought the smell was like candy and cake and flowers all at the same time!

There were angels who liked to fly close the golden pearly gates. They liked to welcome the new angels coming in. The angel gate keepers would always announce when a new angel was coming, and the family of that angel would welcome them in. William was one of those angels. He especially liked to welcome the children and baby-angels who entered Heaven. He would show them around and play with them in Heaven's beautiful gardens and meadows.

One day, the angel gate keepers blew their horns and played their harps, announcing that another angel was coming. "She's coming, Family! She's coming! Get ready!" William saw the family of that angel gather around the gates and he flew in closer to see who it was. He overheard the conversation of two of the family members. One of the angels was a young lady. She said, "Is that my momma?" Another angel, who looked to be about sixteen or seventeen, said, "It can't be! I've been waiting so long to see my momma again.

William guessed that the lady and young man were brother and sister, and their mother was coming. The lady angel said, "Roy, I been here for only over a year and it seems like it's been lifetime!" Roy responded, "I know, Linda! I was so shocked when the gate keepers announced you were coming!" "I was happy to see you, but I knew Mommy and our brothers and sisters would be sad to see you leave!" "So, tell me, what happened with everyone after I left?" Roy asked. Linda said, "Well, Mommy wasn't the same.

She was very sad. We ended up moving to another house and mommy had another baby!" "Another baby?!" Roy asked. "Yes! A little girl!" Linda exclaimed. "Her name is Tracey, and she was Momma's joy!" That got William's attention. Did the Linda angel say Tracey? It couldn't be! Not my teacher?! My favorite teacher?!? William listened closely as Linda and Roy continued to talk while they waited. Linda said, "Yes, my baby sister, and even though she didn't know it, I was so proud of her!" Roy was intrigued.

"Tell me more about our little sister!" Linda continued "Well, she was something else when she was a little girl! Always gettin into stuff! She played dress-up in my clothes and wore my heels. I would do her hair when Mommy went to work. I took her everywhere with me! People thought she was my daughter!" "She grew up and finished school." "She even went to college and became a schoolteacher!" Roy said, "Wow! Really?!?" "She sounds like I would have been crazy about her!"

"Well, as protective as you were about your other sisters, you would have been more protective over her!" They both laughed as Linda continued to tell Roy about their little sister. Linda said, "Yeah, she got married and had two little girls!" Roy was sad that he missed so much after he went to heaven. He had another sibling that he knew nothing about.

William was sure they were talking about his favorite teacher. They had to be. Ms. Adams always talked about having a lot of brothers and sisters and she always talked about her two daughters. William hung his head low, his wings moving slowly back and forth, sad that Ms. Adams' mom was now joining them in heaven. He knew Ms. Adams was going to miss her like his family missed him.

The glorious, golden, pearly gates opened. The angels Linda and Roy gathered around with what appeared to be the rest of the family, waiting to welcome their mother! An older lady flew to Linda and Roy and held their hands. William assumed the older lady was Ms. Adams's grandmother. Another lady with a soft smile joined them. Their wings softly and excitedly waving back and forth in anticipation.

William continued to look on as a beautiful lady entered heaven. She looked just like the Linda angel, just a little older. She had a familiar and beautiful smile. She seemed so glad to see her family. The family gathered around as she entered through the pearly gates. They were hugging her, kissing her, welcoming her into eternal, splendid glory!

The new angel looked over at William. When their eyes met, he knew she was Ms. Adams's mother. They had the same warm smile and tender eyes. With a questioning look on her face, she flew closer to William. William was sure that she was wondering who he was. William flew to her and introduced himself, "Hello! My name is William and your daughter Tracey, Ms. Adams was my teacher!" Mommy said, "Oh yeah?!?" "You're just a little boy! Why are you here so soon?" William said, "Well, I was very sick, and I fought very hard, but it was just too much!"

Mommy said, "I know what you mean! I was very sick too and just plain tired!" "I had lived my life! I was almost 90 years old, and God had been so good to me!" William smiled at Mommy as she continued, "I hated leaving my children and my grandchildren, but I know they will be okay!" William said, "Your daughter was my favorite teacher! She took very good care of me while I was in school, and she taught me so many good things!" Mommy said, "I know! I am so proud of her! I know all the students were blessed to have her as a teacher!"

William shook his head in agreement and took Mommy by the hand, "Let me show you around! It's wonderful here! No sickness! No pain! No more crying and everyone here is family!" William flew ahead of them, excited to show them around heaven. Mommy with her new butterfly wings followed him along with Linda, Roy, and the rest of the family!

As they entered through the golden, pearly gates, Mommy was holding William's hand. Linda and Roy were standing next to them, Linda standing next to Mommy holding her hand and Roy standing next to William holding his hand. Mommy looked at the gates as they were closing. The angel gatekeepers holding the golden handles as the gates were closing. Mommy took one last look beyond the gates. She saw her children. Each one of them. Their faces showed such hurt and sadness. Mommy knew their hearts were hurting. She then looked toward the Light and smiled. She released Linda's hand and from her hand flew five little butterflies.

The butterflies flew through the pearly gates to her children. A butterfly for each of them to remind them that Mommy was never far away. Mommy, Linda, Roy, and William watched as each of the butterflies made it to each one of her children. Each of Mommy's children smiled when they saw the butterfly. Their butterfly. They each knew it was Mommy. They wiped their tears and said, "Hey Mommy! I love and miss you!" Mommy smiled knowing that they would never be without her. Then, Mommy, Linda, Roy, and William turned hand and hand and walked into eternal peace.

About The Author

Tracey was born in Kansas City, Missouri. She began writing at an early age, writing short stories and journals. Tracy is a teacher of special needs children. She has been a teacher for 25 years.

Her first published book is entitled how, "William Got His Wings" and was nominated "Book of the Year" by its publishing company. The story was inspired by one of her second grade students.

Tracy is a best-selling author on two International Best-Selling Anthologies, and she is a writer for the international Best-Selling Magazine, "Unmasking Motivation."

Tracy enjoys creating stories based on her students and her life experiences. She enjoys long walks, anything about history and geography, and planting flowers. Tracy lives in Alabama with her two daughters, Malia and Maya.